No Longer Trapped in the Closet

No Longer Trapped in the Closet

THE ASANTE MCGEE STORY

▲ ▲ ▲

Asante McGee

© 2018 Asante McGee

ISBN-13: 9781979692144

All rights reserved. This book or any portion thereof may not be reproduced or used in any manner whatsoever without the express written permission of the publisher except for the use of brief quotations in the book review.

I would like to thank my three kids for inspiring me to tell my story. Without them, I don't think I would have had the courage to leave. I would also like to thank Terry Brazley, my mother. She's not my biological mom, but blood couldn't make us closer. Thank you for listening to me cry and laugh and for watching me through this journey of my life for the last seventeen years. Schacle Powell, my lil sister, you kept me encouraged and always told me to move forward. I would also like to thank a special person whom I can't name, but she knows who she is. If it weren't for you, I would have not contacted the parents.

Contents

Chapter 1	A Child's Pain · · · · · · · · · · · · · · · · · · ·	1
Chapter 2	When I Thought I Was Safe · · · · · · · · · ·	9
Chapter 3	Safe Haven ·	13
Chapter 4	Adulthood ·	16
Chapter 5	Love, Marriage and Deceit · · · · · · · · · ·	21
Chapter 6	Meeting R. Kelly · · · · · · · · · · · · · · · · ·	32
Chapter 7	Meeting The Trainer (Juice) · · · · · · · · ·	42
Chapter 8	Dildo ·	49
Chapter 9	The Parents ·	63
Chapter 10	Life After ·	67
	Acknowledgments · · · · · · · · · · · · · · · ·	70
	About the Author · · · · · · · · · · · · · · · ·	71

CHAPTER 1

A Child's Pain

▲ ▲ ▲

January 19, 1990, was the day I finally felt safe, safe from all harm, safe from my birth mother. One day when I was ten, my mother sent me to the corner store to purchase loose cigarettes. I'm not sure why my mom thought I would be able to buy cigarettes, but I was not allowed to purchase cigarettes because I was a minor. When I came back home without the cigarettes, my mom punched me in the eye and sent me the neighborhood candy lady to buy some cigarettes. I remember walking to Curran Place crying. There were kids outside waiting for the bus, and one of the kids asked me, "Asante, what's wrong?" I kept walking and crying, not knowing that what I thought were tears was blood coming down my face. When I got to the neighborhood candy lady's house, she asked me what had happened. Why was my eye bleeding? I continued to cry and told her why I was there. I didn't realize I was crying blood instead of tears. Ms. Warren asked me who had hit me. I told her my mom had hit me because I came back without her cigarettes. Ms. Warren called the police to her house and told them what had happened.

My mom came looking for me, and when she arrived, the police were already there. While they questioned me, my mom was yelling at them.

The police decided to go to my house, and I rode with them; my mom followed us. As we were pulling up in the driveway, I was scared—scared they were not going to do anything and make me stay home. I knew if the police didn't do anything, I would get beaten more after they left.

It didn't happen that way. I got out of the car with the officers, and they questioned my mom. She became irate with the officers and hit one of them. Child Protection was called, and more cops came. I had one sister and two brothers, ages six years, one year, and two months. They were all in the living room as the police searched my house. They found toy BB guns, wooden boards, and extension cords, as well as a King knife under her bed. Those were the weapons she used to beat me daily, except the King knife.

My mom was arrested, and my siblings and I were taken to the hospital to be examined. The doctor found evidence of child abuse, and the weapons that were found matched the wounds I had on my body. Most of the markings that were found on me are still on me today—permanent markings on the back of my neck, both thighs, my right wrist, and my right little finger. My grandmother was called to come and take care of us.

At that point, I finally felt safe. For years, my grandmother and aunts knew what was going and had been trying to get me taken away from my mom, but no one would help. About two years prior to my mom being arrested, my grandmother told the insurance man she believed my mom was abusing me. The insurance man called the police. When the police came and asked me questions, all they would say was "We need more evidence."

My grandmother and the insurance guy asked, "What more evidence do you need? When she is dead?"

At that point, I knew no one could help me get away from my mother. I can remember years of being abused, of being beaten just because something red would fall within my sight—she said I was practicing voodoo. She once took a wet, bloody rag with period blood on it from between her legs and stuffed it into my mouth, telling me she was doing this because I loved the color red so much. I was crying, begging her to please stop—I didn't know what voodoo was. If I was watching channel three on TV, she would turn the TV because I was using the number three to practice voodoo. I was eight years old at the time. How could an eight-year-old kid, so innocent, know anything about voodoo or any kind of witchcraft?

I would get beaten for anything. One day she beat me with an extension cord, which left permanent welts on my neck. My godmother bought me new clothes. My mom got mad and cut the clothes up and put them by the mailbox. Then called my godmother, told her what she had done, and laughed about it.

I was beaten with anything and everything she got her hands on, from toy BB guns to wooden boards to extension cords. Every time she beat me, I wondered why she didn't like me. I had three other siblings, and she never touched any of them. Just me. I concluded that she didn't like my dad and that I must have reminded her of him. Every time she saw me, she saw him in me. She would call my aunt and tell her to come and get me; she didn't want me anymore. My aunt would come and get me. But then my mom would change her mind and tell my aunt she was trying to take me from her and threaten to call the police.

Two days before Child Protection came, my mom made me walk to my aunt's house to ask if she could take her to pay her light bill. It was about ten o'clock at night, and I was scared to walk at that time of night by myself.

I knocked on my aunt's door, and she was upset that my mom had made walk to her house at that time of the night. She fed me and gave me a bath. My aunt told me she was not sending me back home that time of night. I was happy to get a decent meal and sleep peacefully.

The next morning, I ate breakfast with my cousins, and my aunt dropped me off at home. I got out of the car with an apple in my hand, and my aunt drove off and went to work. My mom came outside and asked me where my aunt was going.

At that moment, I remembered why she had sent me to my aunt's house in the first place—it was to ask her to take my mom to pay the light bill. I told my mom I had forgotten, and my mom took the apple out of my hand and threw it across the yard. ==We went inside, and she grabbed a knife and aimed it at my chest. I threw my hands up to prevent her from killing me, and she cut my right pinky finger to the bone.==

I didn't know I was cut until I saw the blood. At that point, I felt my pinky finger throbbing, and I started crying, afraid to scream. My mom then panicked, realizing what she had done. I was not taken to the hospital. She just wrapped my finger up with a bandage to stop the bleeding. The following is an account of the incident:

> Officers Farrell Anthony St. Martin and Geraldine Prudhomme responded to the call. They testified they found the child crying, "sort of hysterical" and refusing to go home. They also testified that, in addition to her bruised and bleeding eye, the little girl had bruises around different parts of her body. Due to the condition of the child and her emotional state, the officers decided to call the Child Abuse Division.
>
> The officers also testified that ten to fifteen minutes after their arrival Carson appeared "like a storm trooper" looking for her daughter. Officer St. Martin described her demeanor as loud and

irrational. He thought she might become violent. Officer Prudhomme testified that Carson wanted to take her daughter home, but they would not let her and warned her they were investigating the child's condition.

At some point, the child abuse unit arrived as did at least two of Officer Prudhomme's ranking officers. Officer Prudhomme testified that when she was questioning Asante, Carson struck her (Prudhomme) on the back of the head. She said it took both of her ranking officers, plus two additional officers, to subdue Carson and to get her handcuffed and in a police vehicle. Thereafter, Officers St. Martin and Prudhomme transported Carson to the police station.

Dr. Curtis Turner, the pediatrician who examined Asante after the police took her into custody, was the state's concluding witness. He testified that when he examined Asante in the children's emergency room on January 19, 1990, she had multiple healing wounds and multiple scars on her back and her extremities, including one with the classic loop mark caused by an object like a looped belt or cord. He counted the wounds and found forty-nine. Dr. Turner testified she had fresh bleeding around her left eye and the lining over the white part of her left eye was scratched. He also testified she had a laceration on her right hand on the palmer aspect, the fifth digit, which should have been sutured within twenty-four hours of sustaining the injury.[1]

https://www.leagle.com/decision/19921174598so2d5761990

---

[1]

CHAPTER 2

When I Thought I Was Safe

▲ ▲ ▲

Finally, my siblings and I were safe and out of harm's way. My grandmother was happy to have us living with her. Everything was right—my grandmother kept all of us together. She took care of us as if we were her own kids and not just her grandkids. We were all well nourished, and it felt as if we were living a normal life like everyone else. We had a lot of memories living across the canal with my grandmother, aunt, and cousin. We laughed, and we played, doing everything from making mud pies to playing acorn football with the neighborhood kids. Everyone in the neighborhood knew one another and had permission to discipline one another's children without the other parent getting mad. We all knew to be inside by the time the streetlights came on.

Fast-forward. My grandmother's health started to decline. She was a diabetic, and she started to lose her eyesight. At that point, my oldest aunt was living in Mississippi, and she thought it would be better for all of us to move there so she would be able to take care of my grandmother and us. Living in New Orleans with my grandmother's health declining was hard on one of my aunts who lived across the river. It became a hardship for her because she didn't have transportation.

We moved to Mississippi when I was about fourteen or fifteen years old. My aunt had total control over everything—control over us and my grandmother. Once again, I started feeling that I was being treated like the black sheep of the family. My grandmother was receiving assistance for me—about $500 a month, for me alone. My aunt took control of all the finances. Each month, I would get an allowance of $50. Some would think, Cool, you had $50 a month to do whatever you wanted to do. That was not the case. I had to buy all my own personal hygiene products with that $50. Birthday and Christmas, that was all I got. I asked for a typewriter for my birthday. I was told the typewriter would come out of my $50, and I had to figure out how to get whatever hygiene stuff I needed. It did not take $500 a month to take care of me, but I knew it was not fair for me to have to use my monthly allowance to buy my own personal hygiene. When my grandmother's health was good, she made sure I had everything I needed, and there was no limit. If she couldn't afford it, then she would tell me I had to wait. My aunt was very controlling and wanted everything her way. She was/is money hungry, and I knew she was taking money from my grandmother to support her shopping habits.

I got to the point where I felt I was being abandoned once again. This time I wasn't being physically abused but emotionally abused. My aunt's kids always had the best of everything, and she never treated her kids the way she treated me. She started blaming me for my grandmother's health declining and my mother's being in jail.

I remember having a lump on the side of my breast the size of a fist. I told one of my cousins that I was going to die. She told her mother, and she asked me about it. I was taken to the doctor and found out I had a cyst. They had to remove the cyst, and thankfully, it was not cancerous.

I came to a point where I didn't want to live anymore. I started blaming myself and felt that my family would be happier without me. I was hoping things would get better, but they didn't. I went to my middle school and told my counselor what was going on, that I did not want to stay with my family anymore because they didn't want me there and that they blamed me for my mother's being in jail. That day I was placed in state custody. No one in my family questioned what was going or why I felt the way I did.

CHAPTER 3

Safe Haven

▲ ▲ ▲

The day I left my grandmother's house and entered state custody, I didn't know what to think. I was numb to the entire situation. I couldn't believe that once again I was neglected, left feeling as if no one loved me.

My social worker found a foster home for me. The foster mom had one daughter; I can't remember whether she was her biological daughter or just another foster kid. The foster mom was a hair stylist, so she worked different hours. The living situation was OK; the foster mom didn't mistreat me or anything.

==I had been there for about a week when the girl who lived there invited a male friend over one night, and that male friend bought another male friend over. It was late at night,==

and I remember going into the kitchen. As I was getting something to drink, the other male approached me. The girl had told the friend I wanted him and that I was just playing hard to get. I told the guy to leave me alone. I grabbed a knife and put it to his chest. I grabbed the house phone and called my social worker. I told him what was happening. I was scared and didn't know if I was about to get raped. My social worker drove two hours in the middle of the night to come and get me. When he picked me up, I cried and begged him to never put me in another foster home again.

From that day forward, I was placed in group homes. I was placed in three different group homes during the next two years. My social workers were there for me and made sure I had everything I needed. The last group home I was in was in was in Jackson, Mississippi. Everyone there was nice, and they loved their jobs, and it showed.

While living there, I went to my first R. Kelly concert. One of the staff members asked me and another person if we wanted to go to a concert. I thought, Yeah, right. They are not going to let us go to a concert. They submitted it for approval, and I was able to go. This was my first concert—R. Kelly, Escape, and a group called Solo. I remember seeing R. Kelly performing in a sheer all-white outfit while sitting in a bathtub onstage. I was like, Wow. I had such a good time, and I thanked the workers for giving me that experience.

As weeks, even months, went by, there was an older couple who would come to visit the group home and take us to their church. After church we would go to their house for Sunday dinner. They had a big house that had an elevator in it. They would come and get several girls from the group every weekend and even take us shopping. I felt so special. Why would anyone be nice enough to take strangers into their home, to their church, and shopping?

I was getting close to turning eighteen years old, meaning I would have to transition to living on my own. Before I turned eighteen, my social worker reunited me with my family. I would go visit them on weekends to see how we would get along and see if my staying with them could be an option. Everything was good, and one of my aunts said it was OK for me to stay with her. I was able to reunite with my grandmother and three siblings.

CHAPTER 4

Adulthood

▲ ▲ ▲

LIVING WITH MY FAMILY AGAIN, I felt good. I felt that everything was going well, that we were all getting along. We never talked about what had happened in the past. While living with my aunt and grandmother, I was attending therapy sessions weekly, which was very helpful. I was able to express myself without being judged and knew I would not get in trouble for expressing myself. I attended my senior year of high school in Mississippi. I was the new girl in town and kept to myself.

I managed to make it through my senior year. Graduation day came, and the only people who attended my graduation were my great aunts. None of my mom's sisters attended, even though they were in the same city. I felt upset but didn't let that stop me.

I attended a community college for the fall semester. My grandmother's health was getting worse. She was in and out of the hospital. During my first semester in college, she died. I came home from school one Friday, as I always did, and no one was there. I went across the street to one of our neighbors to use the phone. She told me my aunts were in McComb with my grandmother.

I said, "No, my grandmother is in the hospital in Hattiesburg."

She kept telling me no. Finally, she said, "Your grandmother is dead."

I fainted. I couldn't believe what I was hearing. I had so many questions. I had just called to check on my grandmother that Thursday night, and she had been OK. I couldn't understand why I had to find out about my grandmother's death from a neighbor.

My aunts came home and told me what had happened. I just couldn't believe it. The only person I knew who really cared about me and loved me had died. It was hard for me to take, but I managed to get through it.

A year later, I dated a guy briefly and ended up pregnant. I was close to one of his aunts, who lived not far from where my grandmother lived. Even after I had my daughter, things didn't work out between us. Some said I was a one-night stand, but I wasn't. I could call on one of his aunts to help me with my daughter when I needed to.

One night I was sleeping at his aunt's house with my daughter, and her dad was sleeping over too. Nothing happened between us that night. The next day his girlfriend, Nancy, found out I had slept over, and she went crazy. She was pregnant at the time and came to the aunt's house ready to fight me. Fight me for what? But I was ready. His aunt calmed us down, and Nancy hated me from that day on.

My daughter was one year old, and I packed up everything I had and moved back to New Orleans. I moved in with a friend and her mother and grandmother. They agreed that my daughter and I could stay there until I got on my feet. That lasted about a year.

I ended up in New Orleans homeless with a one-year-old daughter and no one to turn to. I went to the food stamp office seeking help. I told my case worker I had nowhere to go, and she found a transitional home called

Liberty House. I had to go there to do an interview to see if I could get accepted into the program. The program allowed women aged eighteen to twenty-two with children to stay there for up to two years. They taught us basic living skills, such as saving and how to find housing.

My first day there, I learned I had to provide my own living essentials—bath towels, soap, toothpaste, and so on. My first cousin came to take me to get the things I needed. She knew where I was staying and didn't offer to help me. I didn't let that get me down.

The person who did my interview to see if I qualified for the program was a counselor there, and to this day, she is the woman I consider my mother. She believed in me when no one else did. When I entered the program, I knew I had two years to stay there, but I gave myself six months. I left within those six months. I had a daughter who looked up to me, and I had no help from her dad or family.

I got a job at Harrah's Casino as a slot attendant. I moved into the fifth ward with my daughter, and my aunt lived right down the street. Our daughters were nine months apart, so she would keep my daughter for me while I worked overnight.

After we had been living in the house for about four months, there was a drive-by shooting. A young man was killed, and his lifeless body was lying on my porch. My daughter was two years old, and I had to get her to a safer place. I moved the next day.

CHAPTER 5

Love, Marriage and Deceit

▲ ▲ ▲

THIS WAS WHEN I THOUGHT I had finally found love. I met my ex-husband during Essence Festival 2002. A friend and I were leaving the festival. Henry walked up to me and started holding my hand. I was like, Boy who are you? And are you crazy?

He and his friend offered to take us home, so they did. We were sitting outside my house talking, and Henry tried to get in my house to use the bathroom. I told him he was a man; he could whip it out and pee on the side of the house. So he did.

The next day, my friend and I were sitting outside, and I noticed the same car from the night before. I told my friend that it looked like the guy from last night. I went inside to get my phone, because I had left it on the charger. When I got my phone, I saw I had several missed calls from Henry. I called him back and asked if that was him sitting outside my house, and he said yes.

So I went back outside to his car, and we talked. He said he was in the area, so he had decided to stop by. I didn't believe him, but OK.

We ended up talking daily and seeing each other. Less than a year later, we ended up living together, and I got pregnant. I was not ready for another child, but he insisted on us having our son.

I never saw any red flags with him. I was about six months pregnant when the mother of his other child came by. She questioned me and told me they were still together. He had told her I was just a roommate and that I was pregnant by someone else and the child's father had left me.

I thought, Wow, really? She and I were in my living room talking. We tried calling him on his cell phone, but he wouldn't answer. Keshia called another girl Henry was see-ing, and she came to my house to talk. We were all talking, and they both tried to convince me he was no good and that I should leave him alone.

Henry finally came, and the four of us were sitting in my living room talking. Keshia finally said, "Henry, what are you going to do? You need to choose."

At that point, I didn't care either way.

Henry came over to me and touched my stomach and said, "I'm staying with my baby."

We were all shocked.

Keshia said, "Well, I'm still going to fuck him."

And both girls left. The next day they both called me and told me how stupid I was for staying with him. I thought he must really love me to choose me, so I wasn't trying to hear what either girl had to say.

A year later, Henry and I got married, and I eventually joined the army. Throughout our thirteen years together (we were married for eleven of those years), he would yell at me, hit me, and even put a gun to my head while I had my youngest daughter in my arms. Each time he would hit me, he would promise not to do it again, and he wouldn't for a few months. I always made excuses for him, telling myself I had done something wrong, and that was why he did what he did.

I tried to do everything right. When I was no longer in the army, Henry made all the money. We moved to Atlanta in 2006, and things started to get worse. I was working on getting the courts to enforce the child-support order against my oldest daughter's father. I didn't know he was living in Georgia until a year after I moved there. I had him on child support, but he wasn't paying it. I went to see a lawyer, seek-ing help to get the court-ordered child support enforced in Georgia, and I was finally able to get the order enforced.

Lauran, his girlfriend, started getting upset because child-support papers kept coming, and then he was arrested for child abandonment. She took out a warrant on me, saying I was harassing her. I wasn't. She was mad because of the steps I had to take to get him to pay child support.

I was arrested on these false charges, but I never received a court date, and the charges were later dropped because there was no evidence for harassment.

Fast-forward to 2009. Henry met a girl named Lisa and started having an affair with her. I guess things didn't happen the way she expected. She decided to send me a message on Facebook to tell me about the affair she was having with my husband. She said she was in love with him, and I would have the fight of my life. She meant every word.

How dare you tell me I'm going to have the fight of my life when you are sleeping with my husband? They continued the affair for about a year and a half, and she got pregnant. She continued sending me messages, bragging about her affair with Henry and her carrying his child.

▇▇▇▇ ▇▇▇▇ sent you a message on Facebook...
Friday, November 5, 2010 9:39 PM

Top of Form

Bottom of Form

From:
"Facebook" <fbmessage+yat0a2a6@facebookmail.com>

To:
"Asante Shelthia" ▇▇▇▇▇▇▇▇▇▇▇▇▇

Raw Message Printable View

▇▇▇▇ sent you a message.

"ur profile pic on facebook...thxs for the laugh and if i were u i wld invest in a spanxx....u actually do look like a celebrity...jamie foxx as wanda on in livin color...lol...First u were sayin i was a liar and tht ▇▇ was not the father of ▇▇......tht i didnt knw who ▇▇ dad was......i always knw who ▇▇ dad was........ur husband ▇▇.....then u say tht im proud and tht i gt wht i wanted........a baby from ▇▇......no....thts nt wht i wnted......its always gonna b smthg with u.....cause u always wanna b rght......sorry doesnt wrk like tht.......even the best of us gotta b wrg sumtimes......cnt always b wrg.......the main thg u wnt is for us to go away so u cn live ur life happily ever afterr w ▇......lol once again it dnt wrk tht way either.........he has a son by me....whether he hates me or nt.......mad abt it or wht.........doesnt matter wht he wnted.....hes here.... and i dnt understand hw he decides he loves one child differly from the other.......life iis crazy and it definately takes some unknowingly turns.... I hope u cn find happiness.....cause ur husband never seems to amazes me...... hes always definately over the top w everythg......he always knw ▇ was his.........tld u it was just smthg to pacify u.....gt u goin...everyone knws hw easy it is togt u goin Ur a fool for ▇.........u enjoy hm yellin and screamin and actin a fool.....or else u thnk he dnt love u........i told u before.....it wnt last cause u was doin this shit before i came along.......u harrassed the hell out of me....thn whn u sw it again u cldnt take it.......u try to b this big bad wolf and thnk u cn scare everyone off.......but im sorry.....nt one bit do u scare me........i knw wht type of person u r......so does gerald........then he has the nerve to try and question me.... whn he hears someone in the background......teehee its funny.......he doesnt want me but it looks like he doesnt wnt no one else to hv me....im goin to tell u like this...i love ▇ loves me...ur going to hve the fight of ur life because ▇ and me will not going anywhere anytime soon...we are here to stay and u cant do a dam thing about it..."

▇▇▇▇▇▇▇▇▇▇ sent you a message on Facebook...
Friday, November 5, 2010 11:52 PM

Top of Form
Bottom of Form
Top of Form
Bottom of Form

From:
"Facebook" <fbmessage+yat0a2a6@facebookmail.com>
To:
"Asante Shelthia" ▇▇▇▇▇▇▇▇▇▇▇▇▇▇▇▇
Raw Message Printable View
▇▇▇▇ sent you a message.

Subject: lol
"▇▇▇ wnts u to call hm.......he needs to tlk to u.......he has smthg to tell u....Im sure u wnt to knw........▇▇▇ and i was together the weekend before the dna......the whole weekend......he tld me tht the two of u werent....together.....and wld nt b gettin back together for nthg......we slept together all nite everynite until the mornin i left.....well once again

28

███ is about to b a father....which doesnt matter cause he will never knw neither baby.......i wnt b callin hm.....no more contact will i mk. Hv a happy life"

To reply to this message, follow the link below: http://www.facebook.com/n/?inbox%2Freadmessage.php&t=1198298655848&mid=33ece3fG59b23b80G230d3ffG0&n_m=asantecarson%40yahoo.com

Find people from your Yahoo! address book on Facebook! Go to: http://www.facebook.com/n/?find-friends%2F&ref=email&mid=33ece3fG59b23b80G230d3ffG0&n_m=asantecarson%40yahoo.com

▲ ▲ ▲

This message was intended for asantecarson@yahoo.com. Want to control which emails you receive from Facebook? Go to: http://www.facebook.com/editaccount.php?notifications=1&md=bXNnO2Zyb209MTAwMDAxMDI1NTY1OTIzO3Q9MTE5ODI5ODY1NTg0ODt0bz0xNTA0ODUyODY0
Facebook, Inc. P.O. Box 10005, Palo Alto, CA 94303

I knew I should have left, and I tried, but he refused to let me leave. Lisa accused me of manipulating him, saying I was the reason he was not with her and had not been there for her during her pregnancy. She would message me on Facebook, bragging about how she had slept with my husband the entire weekend and everything. She even went as far as getting me arrested for harassing her because she didn't get what she wanted. Of course, the harassment charges were dropped due to lack of evidence.

I finally got the nerve to leave him. I realized he did not love me. If he loved me, he would not have done all those things to me. We finally separated in 2013 and divorced in 2015.

To this day, Lisa still stalks me and harasses me on social media. When I first came out about R. Kelly in 2017, she tried to defame me and stop me from telling the truth. As of today, 2018, she still calls me, and I have recordings of the calls. She has left comments on the social media accounts of friends and known associates of mine.

When Lisa first came out against me, I wanted to cry. I thought, After all these years, why you are so bitter? Why won't you leave me alone?

Henry and I divorced. He married someone else, and she has harassed his new wife. I now have a permanent stay-away order against my ex-husband because shortly after we divorced, he told me he would kill me and then kill himself.

CHAPTER 6

Meeting R. Kelly

▲ ▲ ▲

SEPTEMBER 6, 2013, WAS THE day I met the R. Kelly crew. At first, I wasn't going to go to Club Reign, where R. Kelly was hosting one of the many parties that weekend for the *Black Panties* promo tour. My friend Tammy persuaded me to go, since it was my birthday. The reason I didn't want to go was because he was hosting two parties that night, and I missed the first party. Earlier that day I had met someone in his entourage who invited us to party with them that weekend. I called and texted one of the members, and no one responded to my text or calls.

I ended up going to the second club. I saw one of the guys in his entourage, and he invited Tammy and me to the VIP area. We were asked by one of the members of his entourage if we wanted to hang out with them after the club, and we both said yes. We all left the club together, and we followed them to a restaurant. So many people were there that we didn't even get out of the car. We decided to leave. That night I did not meet R. Kelly. We were invited to attend another event R. Kelly was hosting that weekend, but we didn't go.

It wasn't until January 2014 that I sat down and talked with him face to face. One of the members of his entourage called me and invited me to hang out with them. I met up with his entourage at the mall, and we left and went to the hotel where R. Kelly was staying. We ordered room service and all sat down, ate, talked, and laughed. I was nervous but didn't want to show it. When I was leaving the hotel, he gave me a piece of yellow paper with his number written on it. I was excited, but again, I didn't show my excitement. When I got to my car, I texted him my name, and he replied, "I know who you are." That response alone put a smile on my face.

R. Kelly had a concert in Baton Rouge on February 13, 2014. He invited me, which I was happy about, and we met up at the hotel he was staying in. We rode to the concert together, and I was put in a dressing room until the show started. I was expecting to watch the show from the audience, but to my surprise, I was escorted to sit on the stage.

After the concert, I waited for him in the dressing room. I followed him to the bus. He was talking to some of his workers when some fans came out of the bushes and tried to run to him. But security stopped them.

He got on the bus, and I got in another vehicle and went back to the hotel. I went to my room, and before I could put the key in the door, I got a text telling me to come to his room and the room number. Immediately I got back on the elevator and went to his room.

He opened the door. I entered the room, and he closed the door behind me. I took my shoes off and put my purse on the sofa. R. Kelly lay on the bed on his stomach and told me to give him a massage. I sat on his back and began to give him one. We talked for about an hour, and he asked me questions about myself. He told me that he had many women and that some were like wives to him. He asked if I was OK with that.

I would have been a fool not to think he was dealing with other women. At that time, I didn't think anything would really come out between us as far as being in a relationship. The next thing I know, we started having sex. He was telling me what to do and how to do certain things to him and to address him as Daddy. At first I was like, Daddy? But then I thought, OK, Daddy it is.

After we finished having sex, I got a warm towel out of the bathroom and wiped him off. I put my clothes on and proceeded to go back to my room, but he asked me where I was going. So I lay back down, and we talked some more until we dozed off. Every time he moved, I moved.

Finally, the sun was shining. I got my things and went back to my room. I showered, and he texted me before he left and told me to meet him in the hotel lobby. I came downstairs, and he kissed me on the forehead and gave me a gift, which was a Louis Vuitton bag.

I told him that night I was going to New Orleans to celebrate my cousin's birthday. He left, and I went back to my room to get ready to go to New Orleans.

When I got there, I texted him and told him I had made it. I enjoyed my weekend with my cousins and sister. When I was heading back home (to Atlanta) I texted him: "Daddy, I'm heading back home."

We texted back and forth daily, and there were many times when he wouldn't respond. I never took it personally; I knew who he was, and he was a very busy man.

I was invited to more of his shows. Sometimes I would see him after the show, and sometimes I wouldn't. I would leave the show and go to his dressing room or just go back to the hotel and wait for him to call me. I never got upset when I didn't see him. I knew what to expect.

After traveling back and forth for over a year, I was put to the final test. He flew me to Chicago in March 2015. He had me sit in the hotel for two days before he texted me Friday morning to come to the studio. I took a shower and took Uber to the studio. When I got to the studio, I texted him to let him know I was outside. He called me, and the first thing he asked me was what I had on, I told him, and he said, "Good girl." Next he asked me, "How's the weather?" I told him sunny but windy. He told me his assistant was going to come and open the door to the Sprinter. I said OK. I sat in the Sprinter from about 11:00 a.m. to about 8:00 p.m.

While I sat in the Sprinter, I was talking on the phone with friends. At one point I had to use the bathroom. I texted him, "Daddy, I have to use the bathroom."

No response. As I sat in the Sprinter waiting for him to respond, I was looking for a restaurant or a store where I could use the restroom. I finally I got out of the Sprinter and walked around the corner and found a restaurant and used the restroom. I went back to the Sprinter and continued to sit until I feel asleep.

Around eight o'clock, one of his assistants came to the Sprinter and said, "Mr. Kelly said come inside."

I went inside the studio, and he greeted me with a smile and asked if I needed anything. At this point, I forgot I was even angry that he had me sitting for hours. He was having a party, so there were at least twenty people. We talked for a few minutes until more people arrived. Around four o'clock that morning, I walked up to him and told him I had to leave because I had an early morning flight.

He looked at me with a puppy-dog face, as if he didn't want me to leave.

I asked, "What's wrong?"

He said he wanted me to stay. I came up with every reason as to why I couldn't, but it didn't work. I agreed to stay another day.

I noticed he disappeared with a woman in another room. About thirty minutes later, the woman came out the room smiling to her friends, whispering and laughing. He never came back out of the room that night. I left and went back to my hotel and went to sleep.

The next day when I woke up, I texted him, "Daddy, do you want me to come back to the hotel?"

No response.

Instead of wasting another night in Chicago, I left the very next morning. After I returned to Atlanta, he texted me asking where I was. I replied, "Back home." I had been in Chicago for four days. No response. We continued to call and text and FaceTime, and I was still flying back and forth visiting him.

Feb 13, 2016, 12:07 PM

(312) 925-●●●●

iMessage
Mar 22, 2015, 4:58 AM

> Are you ok! U were looking weak when we was outside.. I hope ur feeling better

> I'm good baby I have been up two days in the studio and then came straight to the show I was exhausted sin me a pic

> You need to stop working so hard and take care of yourself

Mar 22, 2015, 8:26 AM

> Good morning baby

I just don't think you're strong enough to be in my world

But I know you're not a bad person

> Why not?

Because my world is being it's huge and it comes with many rules

CHAPTER 7

Meeting The Trainer (Juice)

▲▲▲

We were still texting and meeting up in different cities, enjoying each other. (Rob always did voice to text, instead of actually texting.) All I ever saw in Rob was R. Kelly, this nice, funny guy whom everyone loved. For two years that was all I ever saw.

A few months prior to me meeting some of the other girls, he told me he didn't think I was strong enough to be in his world. At this point I was confused. I had been with this guy for two years, and out of the blue, he was telling me this. So I asked why not.

He said his world was big and came with many rules.

I told him, "I'm stronger than you think."

On the first day of the *Buffet* tour, in Saint Louis, I met one of the girls. After the concert we went back to the hotel, but instead of getting off the bus, we stayed on the bus. One of his assistants told him he was going to give the guys keys to their rooms. Rob told him he needed a key for his guest (me). The assistant told him he didn't have enough rooms, and Rob told him make it work. His assistant left my key to my room.

It was about three o'clock in the morning, and it was raining hard. Rob and I engaged in all sort of sexual activities on the bus off and on for about four hours. We would take a nap and wake up back at it. I did everything he asked me to do. I did things to him I never imagined ever doing and, although I was not comfortable with it, I acted as if I were.

Around seven o'clock in the morning, he picked up his phone and made a call and told someone to come here. I was expecting someone to come into the bus from the outside. I heard an inside knock and was confused.

Rob said, "Come in." I saw a girl coming out of the room at the back of the bus, naked. He told her, "Bitch, get on all fours."

At this point, I was shocked and confused, and I felt as if I were being punked. I just couldn't believe that with all the noise we were making in the front of the bus, there had been someone on the bus the entire time.

The girl did as she was told, and he asked her a series of questions.

"What's your name?"
   She said, "Juice."

"How old are you?"
   "Thirty-one."

"How long have you known me?"
   "Sixteen years, Daddy."

I was doing the math in my head and was still confused.
   He said, "Good girl. Now get up."

He was still naked, and she sat next to me, with a table between us. Rob sat on a long bench across from us with just a T-shirt on. Juice got the iPad and put some music on.

Rob then called Juice over and said, "Come and suck Daddy's dick."

I was still sitting there, confused.

He then called me over and said, "She's my trainer, and she's going to teach you how to please Daddy. OK!"

He then instructed her to get up and start kissing me. Then he told her to eat me "like Daddy eats you." He told me to start sucking his dick as she performed oral on me.

I was very uncomfortable, but again I didn't show it. He then tapped her to get up. He grabbed my hand and walked me to the back, where the bedroom was, and she followed. He took my hand and laid me on the bed. Juice came in behind us, and it was if she already knew what to do.

I was thinking, This is about to happen. This is about to be my first threesome.

The three of us got in the bed, kissing one another. Rob got out of the bed and told Juice and me to keep going. He sat in a chair in the corner, across from the bed. I listened to his instructions, and then he pulled out an iPad. I noticed he was recording us and started getting nervous. As he was playing with himself, he pulled the blinds up and said, "Oh, this is good. I want everybody to see this."

I looked up and was like, What? Then I noticed the windows on the bus were frosted, so no one could see inside.

He got up and told Juice to leave the room. He and I started having sex, and after we finished, we went back to the front of the bus, where Juice was. I had put my clothes back on, but Juice was still naked, and Rob still had on just a T-shirt.

We continued to talk, and Juice asked Rob if she could eat. He said yes. I was a little confused as to why she had to ask for permission to eat.

About an hour later, we engaged in sexual activities again. About one o'clock, we left and headed to the next city, which was Kansas City. We got there a few hours before it was time for him to go onstage. I saw him before the show and while he was onstage. I didn't see him after the show, which really didn't bother me, because that was a normal thing. I went back to my hotel that night and flew back home the next day. We continued to text and FaceTime each other. Here are just a few texts between R. Kelly and me.

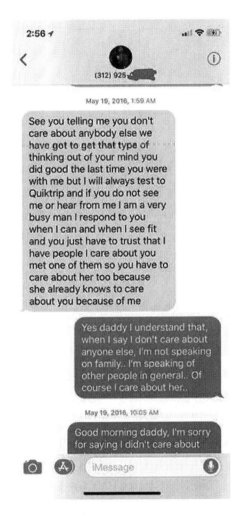

(312) 925-▇▇▇▇
Feb 24, 2016, 10:47 PM

You were all over me at that party as if you were trying to show out for the girl that were next to you you know I am very private never do that again because you have never done that

I'm not the type to show off.. I was drunk and was actually having a good time.. I'm sorry if u feel that's what I was doing.. Yes I know you are a private person and that's why I keep my business to myself

But you didn't keep your business to yourself that night and you are not allowed to use alcohol for an excuse and if that's the case then don't drink around me if you cannot contain your self

Keep it professional unless I say otherwise because you never know what girl who might be around me

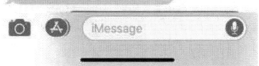

CHAPTER 8

Dildo

▲ ▲ ▲

June 2, 2016, was the day my life changed mentally. I didn't want to believe what I had witnessed and was hoping this was not really happening, but it was. After the Houston show, Rob called me and told me to come to his room. We were staying at the St. Regis Hotel.

I went to his room and knocked on the door. A girl answered the door, a girl I'd never seen before. I walked into the room and sat down. He was sitting on the sofa.

He instructed both of us to come to him. One of us was to perform oral on him, while he played with the other. He moved us to the bedroom. I could tell this girl had done this with him before. I lay on the bed, and the other girl stood next the bed. He went to the dresser where his book bag was and pulled out a dildo. In the back of my head I was thinking, Oh, shit, it's about to get freaky in here; he's bringing out toys.

Rob lay next to me, and the girl started sucking his dick. While she was sucking his dick, he put the dildo in his ass. I was thinking, What the fuck?

He told me, "It's going to be OK, baby. Just lay on Daddy's chest."

The way he got off as the other girl was sucking his dick with the dildo in his ass was nothing like him having sex with females. I couldn't believe what I had just witnessed. The other girl had no problem and knew exactly what she was doing and what he liked. After he nutted, the girl went into the bathroom to get a towel to clean him off. We went back into the living room and sat down on the sofa. Nothing was discussed about what had just happened. We dozed off, and when we all woke up, he told me to order room service.

Someone knocked on the door, and he left us there. I didn't say anything to the girl, and she didn't say anything to me. About an hour later, one of his assistants knocked on the door and told us to come and get in the Sprinter.

I said, "Wait. I need to go back to my room and pack and shower."

She said, "OK, you have ten minutes to do that, and then come downstairs."

I guess the shower felt so good that I didn't realize how long I had been in. I walked out of the hotel to see the bus, the Sprinter, and security were all gone. Rob had given me a number to text when I couldn't get in contact with him. I called the two numbers I had for him, but they were going to straight to voice mail. Then I texted the number he had told me to text only—never call that phone. I later found out it was Juice's number. She never responded to my text.

I made my way to the next city, which was Dallas. I met up with my friend Tonya, who lived there, and I went to her house until he made it to Dallas. We texted back and forth until he got to the venue. My friend and I went to the show together, and he sent one of his assistants to get us and bring us backstage. His assistant gave Tonya a wristband to get all access. The assistant took me to his dressing room. As I sat outside his dressing room, different people were coming in and out, so I never made eye contact with anyone.

Rob walked out of his dressing room and said, "You need to stand when a king enters the room."

I smiled, and he kissed me on the lips and told me someone would take me into the audience ten minutes before he went onstage. His assistant came and took me into the audience, at the side of the stage with two other girls. When I got there, Juice and Cathy welcomed me with a hug. I had met Juice but not Cathy. I remembered seeing her in July 2015 in Connecticut, and I noticed she looked very young. Later I found out how old she was, which meant that when I saw her in Connecticut, she was seventeen years old.

We all watched the concert, smiled, and sang to all his songs. I noticed Juice was texting during the show but didn't know who she was texting. All I could see was that she was in a group text.

I continued enjoying the show, as always. After the show, we all were escorted to his dressing room. He asked if we had enjoyed the show, and then he asked Juice, "How did she do?"

I was shocked and saying to myself, This girl was watching me the entire time. I didn't know I was being watched.

Juice told Rob, "She did good, Daddy. She danced and knew all the words to your songs."

Juice, his assistant, and I waited in the dressing room, while Cathy and Rob went to the back. I started to hear moaning. Juice kept knocking on the door, telling them they were too loud. Eventually, his assistant told us to follow her. She put Juice on the bus and me in Sprinter. I was shocked and was thinking, What's going on? My friend was still there, and I needed to let her know what was going on. So I texted her and told her to follow the bus.

We finally left, and she followed us to a strip club. The only people who got out and went into the club were Rob and his boys. We rode around to at least three different places, and by this time, the sun was coming up. We pulled up to the hotel, and I told my friend to go home.

His assistant told me, "You might want to get your clothes before you end up in the next city with no clothes."

I was like, "What?" So I got my clothes out of the car and got in the Sprinter. We went to sleep in the hotel, and we all left later that day and headed to the next city, which was Oklahoma City.

We arrived at the venue just in time to for him to go onstage. We were escorted to our designated area alongside the stage. We sang to every song, we danced, we all had a good time. After the show we all went back to our hotel.

The next morning, we had to wait in our rooms until someone came to get us and bring us to the Sprinter. That was one of the rules, I was told. I waited until someone got me, which was checkout time, and went to the Sprinter.

He was on the bus with Juice and Cathy, and I was in the Sprinter with two of his assistants. After I had been sitting in the Sprinter for hours, his nephew knocked and told me, "Mr. Kelly wants you to come to him."

I got out of the Sprinter, and he was sitting on the steps of the bus. He asked me for my phone. I told him I had left it in the Sprinter. He told me to get it. As I was walking to get my phone, I was nervous because I had been told he would go through my phone. I grabbed my phone, and as I was walking back to the bus, I noticed he was watching me through the side mirrors on the bus.

He called Cathy and Juice off the bus, and we started walk-ing. Rob made a gesture, and the two of them stopped and hugged me. The four of us walked to a nearby park. A festival or something was going on. There were live bands, other family activities, and food trucks. We walked around for a while and eventually left because too many people started noticing him and were trying to take pictures. I went back to the Sprinter, and we sat there for hours until we finally left that night and headed to Atlanta.

When we arrived, Rob opened the Sprinter doors and told Juice, Cathy, and me, "Welcome home, my babies." We were at his home in the Johns Creek area. He gave us a tour of the home and showed us to our rooms.

After showering, I went downstairs to his man cave–cigar room. We listened to music for a while, and then he told us we could go to sleep and to meet him at a certain time in the Black Room. This was the room where we had sex anytime he instructed us to meet him there. It was called the Black Room because everything in the room was black—all the interior decoration in the room was black, including the bathroom. You never knew who would end up in the Black Room; you just knew to meet him there.

I set my alarm and went to sleep. Later, I went to the Black Room. About an hour passed, and no one came. I stayed anyway. He finally came upstairs and asked how long I had been waiting. Apparently, he had told Juice to tell me he was pushing the time back, but she didn't tell me. Juice, Rob, and I were all in the Black Room. Juice and Rob were sitting in chairs across from each other, and I was sitting on a love seat between them.

After the three of us had sex (which did not include the dildo), I thought, I was really tripping in Houston, and I never wanted to think about that night again. We all went to our rooms until it was time to leave.

Each day I was there, I was given a new rule. One rule was when entering each room, I needed to knock and wait to for someone to tell me to enter. If I was upstairs and wanted to come downstairs, I needed to stomp on the hardwood floor until he told me to come down. One day, I went downstairs and knocked before entering one of the living rooms. I didn't hear anyone, so I didn't think anyone was downstairs. When I walked into the room, Rob was in a corner with Sarah, and I said, "Oh, I'm sorry."

Rob said, "Now what if I was fucking a rabbit? Then I would have had to kill you." I walked back upstairs.

After being in the house for about a week, I was running out of clothes, and I told him I needed to go home and get some more clothes.

He told me "Damn, we are about to leave to go to the studio. Can you go home and be back by four thirty?"

By this time it was about three forty-five. There was no way I could have made it home and back in Atlanta traffic within that time frame.

So he said, "Go home when I'm asleep."

I was saying to myself, You barely sleep.

Rob then told me, "When you go home, bring everything, because you will be living here with Daddy."

I was thinking, Yeah OK, I have kids—who at the time were staying with family and friends for the summer break. I said, "Daddy, you don't like feeding people, and I love to eat."

He told me he didn't want to hear me say that again. He didn't want people to think he wasn't feeding his girls. He asked me what I wanted to eat, and we left to get something to eat. The next time we went somewhere and stopped at a gas station, I bought myself a lot of snacks and hid them in a bag I would carry around.

The next morning, I texted, "Daddy, can I get an Uber to get some clothes?"

He called me and told me to come to the Black Room. I was pissed because I knew I wasn't going to get a chance to get clothes for another day.

Juice, Rob, and I were all downstairs talking with the TV on the ID channel. Juice told me to always make sure the TV was on that channel, because that was his favorite.

Rob told Juice to go check on her sister—he meant Cathy—and to make sure she was asleep.

Juice checked on her and came back and said, "Yes, Daddy, she's asleep."

He took us to another living room that was behind the kitchen, next to the back stairs to go upstairs. He took off his pants, and I started sucking his dick. As I was sucking his dick, Juice took her middle finger and inserted it up his ass. Once again, I was like, What the hell?

He then stopped me and reached into his book bag. Inside was a dildo, this time a double-sided one. I was thinking, Not this shit again. He had the same reaction that he had had in Houston. So many thoughts were going through my head, and I knew I couldn't say anything.

After we were done, he told Juice to make sure Cathy was still asleep. We went back to the main living room and acted as if nothing had happened. We finally went to the studio, only to sit in the Sprinter for hours with no sleep.

There was another girl who would come around; I didn't know why she was living in the house with us. I later found out Sarah was still in college, and she was living on campus. Sarah missed school because she kept trying to call him, but he wouldn't answer.

She started missing school a lot, and no one seemed to care.

Every day a new rule was imposed on me. I needed permission to eat, bathe, and go to sleep. I needed his approval as to what to wear. I was even told during sex to change my voice to sound like a little girl. After I had seen the true Rob, I knew the man I thought I thought I was in love with was not the person I thought he was. I always saw R. Kelly, not Rob.

I was to the point where I had to plan when I was going to leave and how. I had watched an eighteen-year-old girl pull out his dick in front of me and two other people and start sucking on it, and no one seemed bothered but me. All I could think was, What if this were my daughter? How would I feel?

My final straw was when I got yelled at for wearing a tank top. He pulled me to the side and told me to change my shirt. We were all going to the mall while he went to the studio and played basketball. I didn't go with the other girls because I got in trouble for wearing a tank top. He made me go with him to the studio and to the gym. When we got on the bus, he told me the other girls were intimidated by what I was wearing, and he knew it was not going to be good. He went on to tell me I need to start dressing like the other girls in jogging suits.

I told him it was too hot to be wearing jogging suits. He told me I was skinny enough that I shouldn't get hot, and if I didn't have the clothes, then we could make plans to get some. I looked at him as if he were crazy.

I tried to make it until the New Orleans show. That was the show where I had planned to leave. I knew that once I got there, someone would pick me up.

I didn't make it there. Four days before his New Orleans show, Juice and I got into an argument that almost became physical. Juice was trying to make me do something, and I wouldn't. When I didn't do what she asked me to do, she began to yell at me and ask me what was wrong and if I had a problem with her telling me what to do. I said, "Yes!" I remember seeing his aunt and three other girls, and as we were arguing, I was watching them to see if they were going to try to hit me. His assistant ran to him and told him Juice and I were about to fight.

He called me and asked me what happened. We went outside to talk more, and he told me, "You have the black woman syndrome. You don't like for another black woman to tell you what to do, especially a younger black woman."

I told him that was not true. He continued to take up for Juice and tried to make it seem as though it were my fault.

We argued for about thirty minutes, and he started slapping himself in the face, saying he couldn't believe he was arguing with me.

I went to my room, took a shower, and called my friend, who didn't work far from where he lived. I had her pretend she was an Uber driver. When she came, I gave her the gate code to get in. As I was leaving, he looked surprised and asked me if that was my Uber. I said yes and left.

About a week later, he called me and told me I needed to apologize to his guest. And once I apologized, he would send for me. If I didn't do it within a week, then lose his number. I never called to apologize.

CHAPTER 9

The Parents

▲ ▲ ▲

SOME MAY WONDER HOW IT was so easy for me to leave when others stayed. Being abused most of my life, I was able to recognize abuse faster than some who may have not had to deal it. When I left, I knew I had to do something, but I didn't know what. I was talking to someone daily and was telling that person what I had witnessed. I knew the parents of the girls couldn't have known what was going on with their daughters.

So, with a little help, I was able to reach out to the Johnsons and Cathy's mom. I contacted them both anonymously because I didn't want Rob to know what I was doing. When I spoke to Mr. Johnson, I asked him if he knew his daughter was dating R. Kelly and that she wasn't going to school. He told me no and that he didn't care who I was, but he thanked me.

He was going to get his daughter back, and she would not see him again.

I believed him. As for as Cathy's mom, we texted back and forth, but I never called her. I didn't text her from my real number, because I didn't know if I could trust her. I was told they signed their daughter over willingly, so I didn't want them to know who I was.

A few days later, I found out the Johnsons' daughter went back to Rob, and I called them to let them know. They had taken her ID, and they weren't sure how she had been able to get on a plane.

In the early part of December 2016, the Johnsons persuaded me to talk to a reporter off the record, and I agreed. When I spoke with Jim, I didn't reveal my identity. He asked me a series of questions, and a few days later, he asked if I would go on record. Several people had come to him, but they were scared to speak on record. After confiding in a friend, I agreed, and we did a two-hour phone interview about my relationship with R. Kelly.

December 2016 was when I decided to help the Johnsons get to their daughter, since I'd already revealed my identity.

Rob had a Christmas show in Atlanta, and I invited Mrs. Johnson to the show, knowing I would still be able to get an all-access pass. I told her to act as if we didn't know each other. After the concert, we went to his meet and greet, hoping her daughter would be there. But she wasn't.

Mrs. Johnson and Rob talked, but she still didn't see her daughter. I walked up to Rob, we spoke, and I gave him a hug. He asked me why I was acting funny, and I told him I wasn't. He told me to call him when I left there so I could meet up with him. I felt disgusted after hugging him. I didn't have the same feelings I had for him when I knew R. Kelly.

Mrs. Johnson started doing her research and found other girls who had had past relationships with Rob. One of the girls and I grew close—at least I thought we did. We texted and spoke on the phone from January 2017 up until March or April 2018, and then she wanted me to sign a nondisclosure. I felt betrayed. I had never repeated anything we'd discussed for over a year, and now, all of a sudden, my loyalty was being questioned. I did not sign it, and we have not spoken since that day.

When Jim published the article in July 2017, I didn't know it was going to get as much as attention as it did. I received so much backlash from my own peers, calling me a liar. What a lot of people failed to realize was that it was six months after I did the interview before the article was published.

CHAPTER 10

Life After

▲ ▲ ▲

I SEE COMMENTS FROM PEOPLE who think they know, comments saying I'm lying, I just want money, I'm not his type, or I'm too old. Reading these comments attacking me every day once silenced me but not anymore.

One fan dedicated her Twitter to @ me negative things, as if she were hoping I would become suicidal. She called my phone three different times in May 2018, and I recorded all the conversations. To this day, every time something comes out with my name on it, Lisa and Keisha team up and try to go against me in different blogs. She continues to post and share the link with the details of my childhood, saying I caused the injuries to myself. I never knew it was public record, and it's sad for someone to think it's funny to accuse you of lying and causing self-inflicted pain.

No kind of abuse is funny, and people like her are the reason some people don't come forward and report any kind of abuse. All those who criticize me and others like me—I often wonder how they would feel if this had happened to them, their daughter, their sister, or their mother. Would they think it was funny? Age has no limit for being abused.

I can honestly say I feel better today than I did a year ago, or even two years ago. Those who came out and con-tinue to come out against me have made me stronger as a woman and mother. Today I can honestly say I'm happy where I am in life—a successful businesswoman who owns a successful HVAC/plumbing company. I will continue to share my life experiences. Those who doubted me, thank you. Because of you, I was ▮▮▮▮▮▮▮▮▮▮▮ May. 15

More

Replying to @Asante_Shelthia

If you lie on your own mother and have her arrested on false child abuse charges..........what will you do to Rkelly!

0 replies0 retweets0 likes

2. 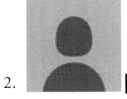 6 May 15

More

Replying to @MegynTODAY @Asante_Shelthia

Anyone who lies on their own mother and purposely have them arrested on false abuse charges...........will definitely try to bury a man like rkelly! You need help and someone needs to make sure of that!

0 replies0 retweets0 likes

ACKNOWLEDGMENTS

▲ ▲ ▲

I WOULD LIKE TO THANK the people who stood by me and believed in me when I first told my story. Schacle, thank you for listening to me and supporting every decision I've made, both good and bad. Terry Brazley, thank you for being the mother I never had. You treated me as if I were your biological daughter. Throughout my journey, you kept me lifted in prayer and always sent me encouraging messages to keep me going. Jade Berry, thank you for being a friend and helping me with some of the edits and making sure my book was at a level it needed to be. Lavell Christin, I know we have had our differences, but through it all, you still showed your loyalty to me, especially when others tried to attack me.

ABOUT THE AUTHOR

▲ ▲ ▲

I WAS BORN IN NEW Orleans, Louisiana, on September 6, 1979. I was abused by my biological mother. I am a divorcée with three beautiful children and one grandson. I've had to deal not only with being abused as a child, but also with physical, mental, and verbal abuse as an adult, by two men whom I thought genuinely loved me. After surviving abuse throughout my life, I continue to remain strong, and I'm regaining my confidence. After coming out about my experience dating and living with the famous R & B artist R. Kelly, I remain calm and continue this journey as I receive so much negative backlash from his fans, my ex-husband's mistress, and trolls. I am now a successful business owner in the HVAC, plumbing, and electrical business.

Made in the USA
Middletown, DE
18 May 2020